S0-BLX-227

Costa Rica

Dear René's Host Family,

We hope you have a Merry,
Merry Christmas, and a Happy
New Year.

We are delighted that you're
going to enjoy René's company
as much as we do.

May this book be a small token
of our eternal gratitude.

René Sr.

Costa Rica

Photographs by Gerhard Eisenschink
Text by Peter Thomas

Artcolor

Cover:
A settlement for plantation workers on the southern Pacific coast.

Frontispiece:
Palm beach in Cahuita National Park on the Caribbean coast.

Following pages:
The beaches of Manuel Antonio National Park are among the most beautiful and most popular in Costa Rica. Wide expanses of sandy beaches are framed by rocky outcrops and rainforest.

© Artcolor Verlag, D-59063 Hamm, 1992
2. edition 1993
All rights reserved.
No part of this publication may be reproduced in any
form or by any means without permission
in writing from the publisher.
Editor: B. Roberts, N. Odenthal
Translator: Gerhard Eisenschink
Overall production: Artcolor Verlagsservice, 59063 Hamm
Printed in Germany 1993
ISBN 3-89261-080-0

This Artcolor book was printed on 100% chlorine-free bleached paper (TCF).

Costa Rica, nature's masterpiece

It has been nearly half a millennium since Christopher Columbus named this unknown stretch of palm trees, surf and sand in Central America »Costa Rica« – the »Rich Coast«. In 1502, he anchored off Costa Rica's Caribbean coast to restock his supplies and to repair his ships which had been badly damaged in a storm. This coast offered everything his weary and exhausted men could ever want: plentiful fresh water, delicious fruits, abundant wildlife and friendly natives. Also, there was the constant lure of gold, the hope for vast treasures hidden deep in the impenetrable rain forests. The dreams of the famous land of gold, »El Dorado« were not to come true for the Spaniards. However, a little less than 500 years later, it now seems that tourism has discovered the real treasures of the »Rich Coast«: a multi-faceted and fascinating landscape, and an abundance of animal and plant species, a biodiversity hardly equalled anywhere else in the world.

Oh yes, Costa Rica! That island in the Caribbean? Or was it that famous beach somewhere in Spain? Not at all! We are not talking about Puerto Rico, or the Costa Brava. The world will soon discover that, in many respects, this is the most interesting country on the Central American land-bridge, this narrow connection between North and South America, bordered by two oceans. Costa Rica's neighbor to the north is Nicaragua and on its southern border it is Panamá.

It all started 120 million years ago. The Central American land-bridge began to slowly emerge from the sea, raised by the titanic forces of two tectonic plates which happened to cause an enormous fault right in this spot. Fractured and bent by forces beyond imagination, the crustal plates rose from the depth to form a mountain range way above sea level. A land connection between North an South America had been formed. Twenty million years ago it was completed, with Costa Rica as its missing link. As the connection between two large continents, Costa Rica has assumed a very special role. The constantly eroding forces of two oceans had confined Central America to a small strip of mountains, a narrow passage, where different cultures and varied animal and plant spheres met. Costa Rica, despite its relatively small size, is a land of many contrasts, and many very interesting sights to see. Evergreen rain forests, sunburnt savannahs and prairies or damp mangrove swamps, high mountains, volcanoes, coral reefs or palm-lined beaches, an abundance of different landscapes and different climate zones form a mosaic of rich and varied environments in Costa Rica. Hardly the size of West Virginia, U.S.A., the country, among other superlatives, can boast of having more species of birds than those found in all of North America combined, and even more varieties of beautiful butterflies than those found in all of the continent of Africa.

»In our country a light jacket can be as important as a swim suit,« a Costa Rican travel information bulletin advises tourists. However, the sun-hungry visitor from a country little blessed with friendly weather should not entertain visions of a vacation of shivering, or of desperate longing for warmer temperatures. Costa Rica is a tropical country and does not know the meaning of »winter«! Yet, even the ever-active tropical sun cannot keep temperatures from getting cooler at higher elevations.

For example, if one wants to explore Costa Rica's Cerro Chirripó, with an elevation of about 13,000 ft./ 4,000 mts., one has to be prepared for temperatures close to freezing and will surely appreciate a warm jacket. Other than that, there is no need to make warm clothes part of your luggage. On the contrary, the coastal plains reliably provide 77–82 °F/25–28 °C air temperatures and 68–77 °F/ 20–25 °C water temperatures and the shade of the tall palm trees by the beach will definitely not go unappreciated. The Central Valley of Costa Rica offers a truly ideal climate. At elevations of approximately 3,000 ft./ 1,000 mts., temperatures range between 65–77 °F/18–25 °C all year round. Although there are no seasons in the tropics, with regard to varying temperatures, the area does experience clear seasonal differences in rainfall. From the end of November to the beginning of May most areas of Costa Rica's Pacific side encounter a dry season. With the ex-

ception of the Caribbean side and the higher mountains, the lack of water takes its toll on the vegetation and the land changes from green to brown. What the northern countries call summer is »invierno«, or winter, for the Costa Ricans, because the rainy season brings a welcome cooling. Normally it does not rain for long, but it is intense. It is undoubtedly a unique experience to stand under the shelter of a palm-covered roof and listen to the mysterious sounds of a tropical torrential downpour. More rain can fall within a few hours than normally falls in a month in many of the countries in the temperate zone. Shortly afterwards, the sun will shine again. It is quite common for clouds to start forming around noon. As they gather, a brief, intense shower is likely in the afternoon and then the rainy »season« is over until the next day.

Costa Rica's incredibly different types of landscape can best be seen on a clear day when standing on the edge of the crater of the 11,260 ft./ 3,432 m high Irazú Volcano. With a little luck, both oceans will be visible. Further south they are a mere 75 mls./ 120 kms. apart. With its narrow shape, Costa Rica seems to be predominantly composed of beaches. Approximately 950 mls./1,500 kms. of exquisite coastline make it quite evident why this small country was appropriately named »Rich Coast«. However, up on the summit of Irazú, you will also be impressed by the high mountains.

Two striking mountain ranges frame Costa Rica's Central Valley, where the capital, San José, is nestled between coffee plantations. From Irazú you will spot far, far below the colorful mosaic of little villages, roads, fields and plantations which make up the heartland of the country.

The mountain ranges are dotted with a number of volcanoes, with quite a few being nearly 9,000 ft./3,000 mts. high. Most of them are dormant at the present time. Their bizarre craters create a lunar type landscape that is reminiscent of their active times, when ashes and lava were a threat to the many settlements and fields on their slopes.

If you should escape the cold northern winter and fly to Costa Rica, you may at first be surprised when looking out of the airplane's window. This brown, burnt land is supposed to host an abundance of animals, moist tropical swamps and evergreen rain forests. In fact, the contrasts within Costa Rica are most striking at the end of the dry season in March/ April. The northwest – Guanacaste – and the central regions in the high mountain ranges look more like dry African savannahs or American prairies than what our stereotype of a tropical country is. As a result, one will find the »gauchos« and »sabaneros« in the grasslands of the Guanacaste province.

With a lot of noise, these »cowboys of Costa Rica« herd their white cebú-cattle through the vast grazing lands. In contrast, one finds a totally different climate, and therefore a very different way of life for the inhabitants, on the Caribbean side of the long mountain ranges of the Central American »Cordillera«. Here, it rains all year long and dense jungle covers the land where it hasn't been cleared for cattle grazing, for banana plantations or for settlements. This is where the Afro-Caribbean culture exists, with most of the original settlers coming from Jamaica. These hardy Blacks were the only people able to sustain the rigors of the jungle. They were the ones who where finally able to build the railroad which connected

the Caribbean to the highlands. Today San José is but a mere three-hour drive from the Caribbean harbor of Limón, but it is a journey into a completely different world. From the modern metropolis, with its busy, light-skinned, Spanish-speaking people, you are transferred to a different Costa Rica, where people have dark skin, speak English and take life a lot easier. »Be happy. Don't worry. Don't hurry.« seems to be the basic philosophy, and a hammock seems to be all one should ever ask for from life.

The ride from San José to Limón reveals the splendor of the impenetrable forests, featuring hundreds of species of trees and many thousands of varieties of orchids. As we leave the Central Valley, (dry from January through May) and make our way up the gentle mountain slopes in a northeasterly direction, we notice that the higher the elevation, the more lush the vegetation gets. Finally, at the highest point of the impressive pass through the Braulio Carrillo National Park, we find ourselves amid the bizarre shapes of the cloud forest. The trees are covered with thick layers of mosses, vines and bromelias. On most days of the year, this very special type of rain forest is hidden in dense clouds, providing extremely humid air. This is the region where mountain lions, jaguars, tapirs and the quetzal live, the latter being the famous, exotic, brightly colored green and red bird of the high mountain forests, whose long feathers were sacred to the Mayans.

During the dry season, the mountain regions remain a green oasis with very rich flora and fauna, and even in the dry northwest there are enclaves which are rich in water and, therefore, a magnet for huge flocks of birds. Where rivers enter the sea one usually finds extensive marsh lands and vast estuaries lined by forests and mangroves. These areas are a haven for white herons, ibises, spoonbills and pelicans. At the Río Tempisque's mouth, water bird concentrations of more than 25,000 birds are not uncommon.

No stay in Costa Rica would be complete without a boat cruise through one of the many wildlife refuges, known not only among scientists, but also amongst all nature-lovers worldwide. The national park of Tortuguero, on the Caribbean side, with its maze of canals paralleling the coast, is a prime example. Its great popularity however, has almost attracted more visitors than the environment can withstand without negative consequences. However, there are plenty of alternatives in Costa Rica. A boat ride on the Río Sarapiquí to the Oro Verde Lodge for example, leads to a very large private rain forest reserve. It is situated directly on the Nicaraguan border in an area that is still completely untouched by tourism. The boat ride on the Río Frío to the Caño Negro Reserve (Refugio Nacional de Vida Silvestre), where crocodiles and anhingas line up on the banks as if on display in a gallery, is another option. A boat trip to the Río Sierpe Lodge, located north of the Osa Península, is yet another alternative, which leads one through the largest mangrove swamp in Central America. How about floating silently by canoe through the mangrove jungle of the Tamarindo Estuary, or on the magnificent Lake Coter at the Coter Eco-Lodge?

Costa Rica has an abundance of such paradises, most of which are well preserved and cared for. The »Rich Coast« managed to protect its valuable treasures in over 46 national parks, biological reserves and sanc-

tuaries, thus making them accessible for visitors. Many other countries will find that, in proportion to their size, they have a lot less to offer in terms of conservation when compared to Costa Rica. Including its private reserves, this tiny country can boast of having over one third of its total territory reserved exclusively for Mother Nature!

Central America, an area so blessed with natural beauty, has undoubtedly been plagued by extremely negative headlines in its recent history. Reports about the dictator and convicted drug dealer in Panamá, who only recently was thrown out of power; a bloody conflict in Nicaragua, which left deep scars on the country; a fragile peace, after a long and cruel civil war in El Salvador, may make one wonder if this is the place for an untroubled vacation? Perhaps the most appropriate and striking answer was given in a cartoon in a Costa Rican newspaper. A little scenario of pictures depicts the political situation in some Central American countries: soldiers are executing a revolutionary; guerillas are firing at the military; armed farmers are fighting with machetes against the hated regime; etc., etc. – and in Costa Rica? Here you find people laughing and drinking, the rich and the poor peacefully united in a little chit-chat and in partying and dancing. The most wonderful thing is that this picture does not at all exaggerate! Costa Rica is in fact the »Island of Peace«, as it likes to call itself. Since 1948 the country has been living entirely without an army, a presumably more than risky situation in an area like Central America. But the concept works. No other country would dare to interfere with peaceful Costa Rica. Serious conflicts with the other Central American countries and with the United

States of America would be the result. Costa Rica is held in high esteem among its neighbors. It functioned as a mediator for peace, and former President Oscar Arias Sánchez was awarded the Nobel Peace Prize in 1987.

The Costa Rican model has become a trend setter and has shown new alternatives, despite the fact that its crisis-troubled, over-armed neighbors are not likely to move in the same direction in the near future. The »Rich Coast« has proven that peace is its greatest wealth. Money saved on military expenses has helped finance schools, hospitals and social programs. With its energetic and consistent development of state and society, Costa Rica was also able to establish peace within its own borders. As a result, clashes between rich and poor are not as big as in other countries of the Third World.

Excellent medical care is available for every member of the population and an effective school system provides for a remarkable, less than 7% illiteracy rate, second only to Chile in all of Latin America. Costa Ricans may boast of having by far the highest standard of living in Central America. These favorable conditions make social conflicts rare and give the country an inner stability. »We have more teachers than policemen,« Costa Ricans proudly comment.

A look at Costa Rica's historical development shows that times were

Following pages:
The Osa Peninsula in the south of Costa Rica features some of the most dense jungle in the country, which seems to grow right into the sea. Many secluded bays and untouched beaches are only accessible from the water.

not always so peaceful. In pre-Columbian days, three different cultures predominated. Their roots can be traced as far away as northern Mexico (Chorotegas), to Brazil's Amazon region (Huetares) in the south, and to what is now Colombia (Bruncas). Wars were plentiful in the region, and head hunting and the taking of captives, whose hearts were torn out of their chests when they were still alive, was common practice. In contrast, the cultural achievements in the area that is now Costa Rica never equalled those of the Incas or Aztecs in the central region of the Andes, nor those of the Mayas, who developed high cultural standards in the middle of the rain forests further north in Guatemala. Costa Rica cannot offer such an abundance of archaeological treasures. However, the National Museum and the Gold Museum in San José still provide some excellent examples of local stone, gold and ceramics crafts of this period.

When on September 18, 1502, Christopher Columbus landed near today's city of Limón, from one moment to the next, a new age had begun. It was to mean suppression and suffering for Costa Rica's native tribes, although it took the Spaniards more than 50 years to systematically explore and develop Costa Rica as a colony. Typical of this time were cruel attacks, killings and pillaging, but also an unbelievable exertion of effort on the part of the intruders when trying to conquer malaria-infested swamps and impenetrable forests. The Spanish liked the pleasant climate of the »Valle Central«, the central high valley, and made it the core area of their new province. In 1563, Cartago was founded, and for centuries this was the capital of Costa Rica.

Through the »Conquista«, the native population was rapidly diminished. Some were killed outright, while others were »missionized« by the Spanish. The diseases they had brought along however, eventually took their toll on the native population. Illnesses, which were completely harmless for the Europeans, caused epidemics among the »indios«. In the 17th century, blood-thirsty bands of pirates made extensive invasions far into Costa Rica from both seas, and the Spanish retaliated in hard-fought battles.

In the early 18th century, the total population of Costa Rica was a mere 24,000 inhabitants, the majority of which still were »indios«, whose numbers kept decreasing drastically. Also, in the 18th century, the Spaniards sustained heavy losses while defending their territory against the English. Operating from Jamaica, the English unsuccessfully tried to incorporate the Spanish province into their dominion. The Spanish colonists also had to endure epidemics of pox and pestilence, as well as huge swarms of locusts which, on at least one occasion, destroyed their entire harvest. Costa Rica was struck by poverty and hardship. The Spanish dream of treasures and gold from the »Rich Coast« had turned into a nightmare. In the end, it was the Church, as an institution, that initiated further development and the founding of new settlements as a result of its ambitious missionary goals. At the end of the 18th century, tobacco left Costa Rica as its first export product. Coffee followed in the 19th century, soon to bring about significant improvement for the country's trade economy. In 1821, Guatemala, together with its provinces – one of which was Costa Rica – declared independence from the Spanish kingdom. After a brief ci-

vil war, the country emerged as an independent republic with the new capital being established in San José. In over 300 years of Spanish occupation Costa Rica did not turn out to be the promised land the Spanish had hoped to find. This remote and hostile land had caused the occupants more trouble than it did good.

This explains why, from the very beginning, Spain's involvement and interest in Costa Rica was fairly limited, a factor which is evident to this day. Throughout their history, the »Ticos«, as Costa Ricans like to call themselves, were forced to solve all their problems by working cooperatively, as they could not expect any help from outside. Racial barriers and class barriers did not develop to the extent that they had in other countries that were closely supervised by the colonial power. One reminder of Costa Rica's discoverer, Columbus (Spanish: Colón), which the Costa Ricans kept, is their currency, called the Colón.

In the second half of the 18th century, the emerging economic growth was beneficial to all levels of society. Poverty decreased as the infrastructure and educational systems were developed. The economy functioned without restrictions by the government and a democratic system evolved on a broad basis. As early as 1848, a school for female teachers was founded, thus giving women access to public jobs. The right to vote was also established for them. Again, Costa Rica's development, so full of promise during this phase, was threatened from outside. The unscrupulous adventurer William Walker had used a power struggle and a war in Nicaragua to take action and subdue that country with an army of mercenaries from California. He then set his sights on Costa Rica.

In 1856, the Ticos succeeded in stopping the invaders on the territory of today's Santa Rosa National Park and drove them off. However, Walker had received substantial support from the Southern states of the United States, who wanted to extend their influence into Central America. It took four years for this threat to end, with Walker's execution in Honduras. The new, up-and-coming country, Costa Rica, had successfully fought back an imperialistic approach of foreign powers. The next attempt on Costa Rica from outside, happened almost unnoticed and without armed forces. Big multinational companies, like the United Fruit Company, gained multi-dimensional influences and started exploiting the country. Foreign capital made Costa Rica a banana republic, an economic structure it retained for a long time, even into the 20th century. Costa Rica's mono-structured economy – exports were based on only a few staple crops – suffered tremendous setbacks through both world wars. The resulting financial dependence still exists to this very day. In the 1940's, expensive social policies exceeded the financial capabilities of the little country and inflation, corruption and general dissatisfaction resulted. In the Civil War of 1948 people fought and defeated their government. The following year, 1949, a new constitution was approved, while the army had been permanently abolished on December 1, 1948.

Nowadays, when Costa Rica is called »The Switzerland of Central America«, it is true in many respects. Political neutrality, a relatively high standard of living, the special status of an extremely small country and an excellent reputation among its neighbors, account for similarities with the European country. But, if one should

expect to find Swiss precision and punctuality in Costa Rica, one would quickly learn better. Here you are in the heart of Central America, in a climate that does not know cold weather, in an area where, during the whole year, fruits literally grow into people's mouths. It is no surprise that this is the land of the happy-go-lucky attitude?

So if your »reserved« hotel room is not ready, the promised rental car is a week late, or the important connecting flight has been cancelled, then try to smile and remember, you are on a vacation where everything is different. Perfection is only for the gods. You can take comfort in the knowledge that your possible anger will be more than compensated for by the outstanding friendliness and openness of the Ticos, who will go out of their way to make each visitor feel more than welcome.

Luckily, Costa Ricans have so far managed to avoid encountering the negative side of tourism. With the help of God, and proper tourist management, this will hopefully remain so for a very long time to come! When you, as a traveler, approach a Tico, a friendly smile and perhaps a little Spanish will help you communicate with him/her. You will see how proud he or she is of the fact that a foreigner has come a very long way to see this great little country. The eyes of every Tico and Tica will shine and their hearts will be filled with pride when you tell them of the many exotic animals you saw, of the exciting and different volcanoes and of the unbelievable forests that are so much bigger and greener than at home. Oh yes, they do love their little country and they have many good reasons to justify their pride!

Costa Rica's population is fairly homogeneous. The descendants of

the Spanish »conquistadores« make up the greatest part (97%) of the population. As light-skinned mestizos, they dominate – visually as well as economically – the appearance of Costa Rica. A mere 0.2% of the population of three million may be called »indios« – the true native Costa Ricans. Dispersed in 18 reservations, they live mainly in the rain forests, being subsistent farmers like their ancestors, and they are rarely found outside these isolated areas. With little government support, lacking true equal rights and without an identity as a people, they live at the fringe of Costa Rica's society. The Afro-Caribbeans also make up only a small portion of the population. Black Ticos live almost exclusively on the Atlantic coast. In addition, a small percentage of the population is of Asian – predominantly Chinese – origin. A hundred years ago they came to the country as cheap labor forces for the railroad projects and are now mostly owners of bars, restaurants and small hotels dispersed throughout the country.

The true temperament and vivacity of the Ticos is best revealed when they dance »salsa«, »merengue«, »calypso« and others, names that sound like whirling feet and bodies caught in motion. These dances have an endless energy supply in their rhythms, overcoming a whole continent – and even more so our little Costa Rica. And so they dance, from the hot streets of Puntarenas on the Pacific, to the humid bars of Limón on the Caribbean, where reg-

Following pages:
Manuel Antonio Beach in the early morning light.

gae joins in with its pounding locomotion. Partying and dancing appear to be a top priority, as there is always a reason for partying.

In 1986 the new highway from San José down to the Caribbean coast, »Carretera de Guápiles,« was completed. It was a long desired and much needed economically important transportation link. Right after it was opened, the first traffic jam was unavoidable. Whole villages came to celebrate the inauguration of the highway as the end of their isolation. They made a continuous dance floor out of the lanes, and cars had to slowly find their way through the huge party. The right spirit, also of the liquid variety, is an essential ingredient for parties. Breweries in Costa Rica offer five different brands of delicious beer that visitors enjoy with equal »gusto«. German brewers emigrated shortly after the turn of the century, ready for a cultural exchange with the New World, and this resulted in very successful products. Brand names like »Pilsen« or »Bavaria« reveal the roots of these delicious drops.

What kind of work do the Ticos do? A trip through Costa Rica reveals coffee plantations, trucks loaded with bananas, numerous oxcarts with huge wheels and archaic looking beasts pulling the loads. One will not find smokestacks, industrial plants and assembly lines, that could disturb our idyllic view of this tropical paradise. For Costa Rica however, this means a strong dependence on agricultural products, whose prices fluctuate considerably on the world market. The country almost completely lacks mineral deposits to provide jobs in the industrial sector. Only in the central highlands are there some factories and manufacturing plants. Otherwise, Costa Rica is an agricultural country. The coastal lowlands of the Atlantic are dominated by vast banana plantations. At higher elevations coffee is typical, and in the dry northwest, cattle farming is the only source of income, besides growing rice and sugar cane. Setbacks in one sector can hardly be buffered by the few others, thus creating a problematic situation. For example, in 1983 the United Fruit Company was no longer able to continue producing its huge mono-cultures in the Pacific area profitably, due to high labor costs. It therefore completely withdrew its operations from Costa Rica and left behind many burning socio-economic problems, as whole regions depended on the jobs they had generated. Now that grass has grown over the old packing facilities and shipping quays, the banana companies are coming back. A worldwide price gain for the yellow tropical fruit makes it again seem feasible to destroy rain forests for even bigger plantations.

With an economy that is basically mono-structured, and an industrial sector that is little developed, Costa Rica began looking for jobs in the tourist sector during the past two decades. Since North Americans and, more recently, Europeans have discovered this hidden paradise, the monies spent by foreign visitors have become an increasingly important source of income, surpassing coffee and almost equalling bananas. So far, Costa Rica has been wise enough not to overdo touristic development.

Fortunately, the country lacks huge hotel structures, the imposing and hideous types, that have turned many a dream beach in the world into a visual and ecological nightmare. Costa Rican laws dictate that buildings by the beach cannot be higher than the natural vegetation. The fencing off of beaches, as a private terrain of some tourist ghetto, will never be possible in Costa Rica. The first 150 ft./50 mts. from the average high tide mark are always public, and private property can be acquired only beyond that boundary, even though the next 490 ft./150 mts. have to be free of stone or concrete buildings or walls, and can only be developed under government approval. So the future looks bright for those of us who want to walk along the beach for hours, from bay to bay, limited only by Mother Nature herself, through capes, cliffs and the mouths of rivers.

»Costa Rica is more than just a vacation in the sun. It is an education in Nature's classroom,« says the brochure of a local tour operator, thereby giving the country the right description. Despite all the wonderful, tempting beaches, the traveler should not forget he is in one of the world's leading countries for diverse landscapes.

Though Costa Rica's roads may slow the traveler down a little, the distances are short enough for a program full of contrasts: from a coral reef to a volcano, from a prairie to a rain forest. In other parts of the world one would have to travel from country to country to see such contrasts. If the average tourist's interests are not focused only on sun, sand and sea, but also on Costa Rica's nature, with its national parks and sanctuaries, it will help boost the trend of setting aside a growing number of areas for nature and the development of ecotourism. Only time will tell if these areas will be negatively affected by growing numbers of visitors. The national parks of Tortuguero and Manuel Antonio, two of Costa Rica's biggest attractions, are examples of the resulting problems: too many people are concentrated in too small an area of the park. Visitor management, planning and directing where they go, as well as off-limit areas for vegetation and animals, are definitely in order.

The need for a policy to establish more reserves in Costa Rica and to properly handle the growing number of visitors is quite evident – especially on private lands where there is no involvement of public conservation agencies. Nature lovers can provide the financial basis for rain forest protection. In fact, the »green heart« of the tropics is severely threatened outside of the national parks and existing reserves. Due to their easy accessibility, Costa Ricans cut down more of their forests than in any other country in Central America, a dismal fact that is in sharp contrast to the ideals of conservation so well displayed in the many national parks. For economic reasons, the forests are being sacrificed for grazing land or for the logging industry.

However, it is also in Costa Rica where a few very interesting model projects have proven that rain forests can be more profitable when they are turned into a reserve for ecotourism. The Rara Avis Biological Station is an internationally known example of the successful integration of research and ecotouristic development of an otherwise inaccessible jungle, together with low impact harvesting of seeds and fruits. Furthermore, the Oro Verde Lodge, on the Sarapiquí River, or the Ecoadventure Lodge, at Lake Coter, have saved rain forests from being cut down, due only to private initiatives. In many other areas of Costa Rica similar projects have started to materialize. A growing number of visitors, eager for first-hand nature experiences amidst the evergreen »ocean of leaves«, make these attempts a promising conservation alternative – despite, or even because of, their economic background. When considering the worldwide situation regarding the rain forest, this is only a promising first step

to show the way. Many, many more will have to follow.

The question as to wether or not tourism will ultimately be a help for nature and a cure for Costa Rica's fragile economy, has yet to be answered. Too many other underdeveloped countries have already dreamt this dream, and then large hotel companies have destroyed their beaches, and life has became too expensive for the locals. Too many visitors have driven off the animals and, in the end, all they have gained were a few glossed-over figures in their economic statistics. Costa Rica has gotten off to a good start, and clear regulations exist, in order to avoid repeating many of these same mistakes. In many ways, the future is up to us, the visitors to Costa Rica. We must commit ourselves to low impact tourism, to a respectful attitude toward the people and the culture of this country, and to ecotourism, with a serious interest in the protection and conservation of Costa Rica, »Nature's Masterpiece«.

Following pages:
Costa Rica's coastline is 1,500 kms/9,000 mls. long. The greater part lies on the Pacific side, where sandy beaches alternate with rocky headlands.

Small wooden houses, in which large families often live, dominate the landscape in Costa Rica. Ticos are very sociable and life takes place outdoors, right before the neighbors' eyes.

Preceeding pages:
Dusk over Rio Sierpe Lodge north of the Osa Peninsula. Here, the largest mangrove area of Central America, a fascinating maze of canals, is to be found. Many rivers in Costa Rica have flooded estuaries which attract a profusion of animal life.

Following pages:
A settlement for plantation workers on the southern Pacific coast.

Mixed cultivation in the Central Highlands where, at an elevation of around 1.000 mts/ 3,000 ft., sugar cane, tropical fruits and ornamental plants are grown alongside Costa Rica's staple commodities: bananas and coffee.

Costa Rica's agriculture is not highly mechanized. Animals are still widely used and manpower continues to play a major role. A farmer is never without his machete, with which he takes up the incessant battle of keeping the jungle from overgrowing his fields.

Following pages:
The Central Valley ist Costa Rica's economic heartland. Fertile volcanic soils (the back of the picture shows the Turrialba Volcano) are ideal for the famous Costa Rican coffee.

Churches in the varied landscape of the highlands: The Spanish »Conquistadores« settled here in great numbers and introduced Christianity to the country.

Picture at right:
A small settlement on the slopes of the volcano Turrialba in the Central Highlands.

The cathedral »Nuestra Señora de los Angeles«, in the former capital Cartago, is an important pilgrimage destination for Catholics. Every year on the 2nd of August, a procession from San José to the church, in which there is a picture of Mary in a frame decorated with gold and precious stones takes place. Thousands of people join in this procession, which has become something of a national festival.

Old fassades in a modern city: Not much is left of the Spanish colonial architecture. The only example in the capital, San José, is the post office on Avenida 1 (picture at right). The city is among Central America's most important economic centers. The noise and pollution present there provide a marked contrast to Costa Rica's natural paradise.

Following pages:
Costa Ricans love colors, evident in both their clothing, as well as their houses. Turquoise, blue and green are especially popular.

A chain of fascinating volcanoes borders the eastern side of the Central Valley. The best known and most accessible are the 3,430 m/11,253 ft. high Irazú (picture top of page), and the 2,700 m/8,858 ft. high Poás (picture bottom of page).

Preceeding pages:
The Arenal is not only Costa Rica's most active volcano, but one of the most active on earth. At intervals of only a few hours, it regularly spews out ashes and glowing magma. Particularly at night, this is an extraordinary spectacle that can safely be watched from its base.

The almost 2,000 m/6,561 ft. high Rincón de la Vieja Volcano is situated in the dry northwest of Costa Rica near the Nicaraguan border. It offers a spectacular view of the Pacific Ocean in the west, Lake Nicaragua in the north, and the rainforests of the humid Caribbean side in the east.

Picture at left:
A dormant minor crater of Poás, now a blue lake surrounded by dense jungle, presents a stark contrast to the inhospitable landscape of the main crater.

Costa Rica's mountains are overgrown with dense rainforests and cloud forests at higher elevations. Numerous rivers begin in this zone.

The cloud forests in the »Cordillera de Talamananca« (Top picture).

The idyllic waterfall of Rara Avic (Bottom picture).

The Braulio Carillo National Park (Picture at left).

The diversity of life in the tropical rainforest is unequalled anywhere else on earth. The permanently moist, warm air provides optimum growing conditions for plants and a rapid biological turnover – a permanent cycle of growing and decomposing. Many plant and animal species in this green maze have eluded discovery by scientists to this day.

Preceeding pages:
Mountain rainforest of the Ecoadventure Lodge: The clearly demarcated layers of growth are indicative of the fight for light in the jungle. Shaded by the canopy of large trees, tree ferns and smaller plants grow in the dim light, forming an intermediate layer of growth. Beneath this layer, only very sparse vegetation grows on the almost dark ground.

Preceeding pages:
Dawn descends upon the forest, but the jungle never sleeps. A concert of hundreds of exotic sounds proves there are at least as many animals active by night as there are during the day.

Be it the orchids, parrots, butterflies, locusts, coatimundis, monkies, iguanas, anhingas or poison-arrow-frogs, Costa Rica's diversity of plant and animal life is unequalled. This small country hosts 850 species of birds, 1100 species of orchids and 2700 different butterflies.

Nestled in the mountains of Costa Rica's north are Lake Arenal and Lake Coter, partly lined by rainforest. The mountains in this region form a distinct division between climatic zones: the dry northwest and the humid Caribbean side of Costa Rica.

Climatic contrasts: Guanacaste, Costa Rica's northwestern province, has a clearly marked dry season. The land calls to mind African Savannahs and steppes, where the vegetation has not been cut down for grazing land.

Here, in the home of the »gauchos« and »sabaneros«, the Central American cowboys, cattle breeding is the main source of income.

Following pages:
A tropical beach at evening. Kilometers of palm-lined beaches are typical of Costa Rica's coast. A balmy breeze from the sea, the whistling of the wind in the trees, the sound of pounding waves and a concert of hundreds of cicadas are the essence of a tropical evening.

Children of the Caribbean coast. This area of Costa Rica is home to the Blacks, whose culture is quite different from that of the rest of the country.

Idyllic Caribbean beaches: Black Beach at Cahuita. Bottom pictures: The popular beach of Playa Chiquita.

Preceeding pages:
Columbus must have had golden treasures in mind when he came to this coast and called it »Costa Rica«, the rich coast. For the traveler, the wonderful beaches have become the country's true gold. Low impact tourism, without gigantic hotel complexes, will hopefully keep them in their pristine state.

South of Puerto Viejo: It is still possible to stroll along the secluded beaches from bay to bay as a contemporary Robinson Crusoe.

Following pages:
Wild Caribbean coast: Although the ocean provides high waves for the surfers, there are protected areas in bays and behind reefs that are ideal for swimming and relaxing in the shade of palm trees.

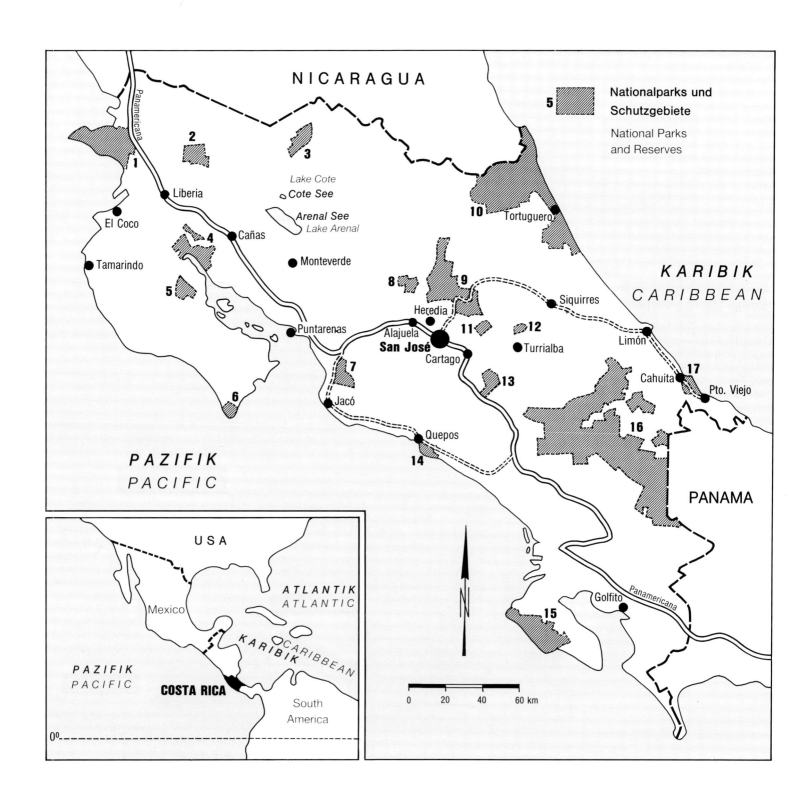

National Parks and Reserves

1	Santa Rosa	**7**	Carara	**13**	Chirripó
2	Volcano Rincón de la Vieja	**8**	Volcano Poás	**14**	Manuel Antonio
3	Caño Negro	**9**	Braulio Carrillo	**15**	Corcavado
4	Palo Verde	**10**	Tortuguero	**16**	La Amistad
5	Barra Honda	**11**	Volcano Irazú	**17**	Cahuita
6	Cabo Blanco	**12**	Tapantí		

ABC of National Parks and Reserves

National Parks

Barra Honda – A karst land (i.e., a chemically eroded limestone area) which is strongly influenced by both the rainy and dry seasons. Under the vast savannahs and white rock escarpments there is a huge, virtually unexplored system of caverns.

Braulio Carrillo – The main highway connection from San José into the Caribbean, »Carretera de Guápiles«, runs right through this relatively unexplored park. The road leads through various types of tropical vegetation at different altitudes, including the cloud forest region. You can either get a fascinating view of forested mountains and deep gorges or you are surrounded by clouds and thick fog, the likes of which you would never expect to find while on a tropical vacation.

Cahuita – A Caribbean dreamland with long, white, sandy beaches lined with rows of swaying palm trees. The only active coral reef in the country, ideal for snorkeling, is here. Dense jungle comes close to the ocean and is accessible by a trail along the coast.

Chirripó – With an elevation of 12,526 ft./ 3,819 mts., it is the highest mountain peak in Central America. Chirripó was even covered by glaciers during the Ice Age. Lakes, páramo (a special type of vegetation adapted to great heights), a cloud forest with an abundance of plants and animals and an outstanding view of the largest continuous jungle region of Costa Rica, all help to make the strenuous hike up the mountain well worthwhile.

Corcovado – Dense tropical rain forests with huge trees, framing a lagoon in the middle of the park. Corcovado has wonderful but fairly inaccessible bays and beaches on its western side. The remoteness and inaccessibility of the Corcovado Park on the Osa Peninsula, has left the natural fauna and flora almost untouched up to present times. Unfortunately, there is now a threat of gold exploration taking place, using large machinery.

Isla del Coco – 320 mls./500 kms. off the coast of Costa Rica in the Pacific Ocean, is the largest uninhabited island of the world and a natural paradise, both over and under the water. It is believed that pirates hid their treasures on this island, which is presently quite strictly protected and guarded.

Manuel Antonio – This tiny park is made up of some of the most beautiful beaches in Costa Rica, embedded between little islands and rocky reefs. On weekends, it is a very popular spot for the native Costa Ricans. Dense jungle, partly accessible by trails, comes very close to the sea. Colorful crabs and frigatebirds are just two examples of the rich fauna that is easily found here.

Palo Verde – This park is found on the delta of the Tempísque River, and is one of the best spots for bird watching, anywhere in the world. The river is home to many crocodiles, some measuring up to 16 ft./5 mts. in length. The swampy areas of the park, with their dense mangroves, are subject to dramatic changes in tidal water levels. The area is fringed by savannahs and dry forests.

Santa Rosa – Extensive tropical dry forest, very unique to Central America. This is the site of the historical battle against William Walker and his band of filibusters. The park has savannahs, gallery forests and mangrove jungles. Giant leatherback and Ridley sea turtles lay their eggs on its remote beaches.

Tortuguero – This maze of canals in dense jungle has rich flora and fauna. The beaches are nesting grounds for rare sea turtles. Access is over 50 mls./80 kms. of canals, parallel to the Caribbean coast, and offers a rewarding boat trip on which one is likely to see white herons, toucans, parrots, turtles or iguanas. Due to its popularity, the park urgently needs protected zones and visitor limitations to its eastern sector. The remote western part is also affected by poaching and illegal logging.

Irazú Volcano – The peak, with its five craters, provides probably the best panoramic view in the country. On a clear day, if you arrive early enough, both oceans are visible. The ride up, either by car or on horseback, leads into progressively cooler zones. Green pastures with dappled cows are more reminiscent of Switzerland than of a tropical country. On the way up, one passes the highest restaurant in Central America.

Poás Volcano – A visitors' deck provides a great view of the crater 1,000 ft./ 300 mts. below. This huge structure, 1 ml./ 1.6 kms. in diameter, houses the biggest geyser on earth, with water columns up to 300 ft./100 mts. that are, however, very rarely seen. An older crater is hidden in the dense jungle and is filled with a lake. High humidity all year round, accounts for the thick layer of vines, mosses and epiphytes on the trees.

Rincón de la Vieja Volcano – The active volcano with nine craters around its peak, boiling mud cauldrons and thermal springs at its base, is accessible only by a dirt road. Its slopes are covered with both dry and humid rain forests and African-type savannahs.

Reserves, National Monuments

Isla del Caño – Off the coast of Corcovado, this little island is completely overgrown by jungle. Its waters offer some of the best snorkeling or scuba diving in the country. With its huge stone boulders, it hides one of Costa Rica's greatest archaeological secrets.

National Monument Guayabo – The most important archaeological site of the country displays sculptures, walls and aqueducts, dating as far back as 800 A.D. Only about 8% of the total site has been excavated to date.

Cabo Blanco Absolute Reserve – A bizarre-shaped, rocky coast, wide, sandy beaches, and typical examples of tropical dry and humid forests, frame this remote sanctuary for large colonies of seabirds. The region is strictly protected and only accessible with special permits.

Caño Negro – The amount of precipitation during the dry and rainy seasons has a strong impact on this flat marsh land, which is a haven for water birds. During the rainy season it becomes a vast lake, but it is dried out the rest of the year. Access is best by boat via Río Frío, close to the Nicaraguan border.

Tapantí – Mountain rain forest, rich in plant and animal life. Several little rivers cross the impenetrable jungle that is accessible only by a few trails. The reserve is easy to reach from Cartago or San José by car.

Private Reserves

Coter Ecoadventure Lodge – This private reserve near Lake Coter is surrounded by a mountain rain forest and cloud forest with many well established trails next to a beautiful lodge that accommodates nature lovers. Special tours for bird watching, as well as many other activities such as boating, fishing, horseback-riding and windsurfing on both Lake Coter and nearby Lake Arenal are all offered. Trips to Arenal Volcano, towering on the eastern shores of the lake, offer spectacular views of the frequent eruptions with loads upon loads of ashes and magma being ejected high into the air.

Monteverde – Well developed cloud forest reserve with nature trails through tropical mountains, rich in plant and animal life. The reserve was founded in 1951 by Quakers who emigrated from the U.S. Having become a classic expample of rain forest conservation, it is today a »green island« in an almost completely logged mountainous region. As a result of its popularity, in part due to the »Children's Rain Forest«, the trails sometimes are overcrowded.

Oro Verde – A large rain forest reserve on the Sarapiquí River, it is located in one of Costa Rica's most remote areas and has the feel of the Amazon River. It is a private conservation area and can only be reached by boat. Excursions from the jungle lodge lead into the rain forest and out onto the river near the Nicaraguan border.

Selva Verde – Located near Puerto Viejo by the Sarapiguí River, this large finca is comprised of dense mountain rain forest that is now part of a reserve for touristic use. Two lodges provide accommodation. A number of marked trails lead through the forest. Maps, as well as tours with private guides, are available.

Rara Avis – This biological station is in the middle of a remote rain forest area neighboring Braulio Carrillo National Park. The wooden jungle lodge next to an enchanting waterfall provides comfortable accommodation, hidden from the civilized world. The forest is rich in species and is partly accessible by trails. Donald Perry did his famous research on the canopy of the rain forest in Rara Avis and discovered many unknown animals and plants. On the way to Rara Avis it becomes more than obvious what would have happened to the forest had it not been saved by private initiative: it would have been cut for grazing land that has already eaten away the natural vegetation in the direct nighborhood of the biological reserve. Today the station is recognized as an internationally acclaimed management model, which affirms that low-impact use of the forest, including ecotourism, is economically more feasible than cutting it down for grazing land.

La Selva – The biological station provides fewer facilities for tourists than, for example, Rara Avis because it permanently hosts a great number of scientists and students who use its library, study rooms and laborataries. Accommodation is rustic with bunk beds in most rooms and only a limited number of private rooms. A great number of trails, well improved in some places, muddy and difficult in others, lead far into the jungle.

An active vacation in Costa Rica

Costa Rica has miles/kilometers of unspoiled beaches, inviting the traveler to swim, relax or do nothing. All year long, warm water and a tropical sun, that knows no winter, make Costa Rica an ideal destination for beach life.

The country has so much more to offer, however. Here is one of the most interesting areas in the whole world, geographically speaking, a jewel, a natural paradise, framed by two oceans, much like a pearl in an oyster. And so, in the past few years, Costa Rica has developed a special type of active, nature-oriented vacation. The country has always been a mecca for bird watchers, butterfly and/or orchid specialists. This natural laboratory for biologists and scientists has been adapted to the interests and needs of the average tourist. When, for example, you are on a guided tour through the rain forests at the Ecoadventure Lodge, at Lake Coter, or at the Rara Avis Biological Station, you need not be intimidated by Latin names or sophisticated, scientific explanations of flora and fauna. The tours here are mainly designed to help visitors from other parts of the world become familiar with the phenomenon of a »rain forest« and the fascination of a »sea of green« which incorporates the richest and most diverse ecosystems of our planet, in as simple a manner as possible. Experience is what it is all

about: to see, to feel, to smell, to taste, to become a part of the forest, and to be aware that the rain forest's life originates very much from the rain. As you wade through the red mud in rubber boots, and protect yourself from the pouring rain in ponchos, or under a huge leaf, you become a significant part of the jungle environment.

Let us not forget Costa Rica's tropical rivers. They come from the moist mountainous areas, where most of their upper reaches feature exciting white water. Costa Rica has always been a well-kept secret among

kayakers and rafters, and river names such as the Pacuare, Corobicí or Reventazón are all well-known. A challenging, but at no point dangerous, rafting trip through the jungle is provided by San José-based tour operators. Excellent safety standards and an exciting day are certainly assured.

The Sarapiquí River is located in the different climatic zone of Costa Rica's dry northwest. It is particularly well-known among nature lovers because it provides an opportunity to take a smooth boat ride along the gallery forest that lines its banks. From the boat, there are plentiful occasions to watch the rich animal life that gets drawn to that green oasis in an otherwise dry environment. Herons, parrots, toucans iguanas and

many more rest or feed in the big trees as one drifts silently by.

Costa Rica's rivers have yet another facet to them. Their deltas, dammed up by the high tides, often turn into vast marsh lands, a maze of canals and a paradise for water birds, turtles, iguanas and even crocodiles. From a boat the whole scenario moves by as in a movie. Hopefully, the trend toward electric motors and canoes will keep pace with the growing interest in such trips. Nature lovers, armed with binoculars and telephoto lenses, are usually amazed at how many more animals their native guide will discover in the dense vegetation with merely his naked eye.

Horse-lovers will also be drawn to Costa Rica. Trekks on horseback, up to and into the craters of volcanoes, through the rain forests and other diverse landscapes, provide the type of riding that cannot be done at home. Surfers will find the swell of a lifetime on the Caribbean side, or on the southern Pacific coast. Windsurfers, however, are rarely seen on the ocean, though protected bays offer excellent opportunities. For them, there are two hot tips further inland: Lake Arenal and Lake Coter. Arenal, with its often extreme gusts, is one of the best areas in all of the Americas (equalled only by The Gorge in the United States), for the experienced windsurfer.

Ecotourism – and what it's all about

(by Joanne Carter)

Over the past few years the world has witnessed the phenomenon of Ecotourism come to life, and Costa Rica may well be considered the world's leader in this field. There seem to be various theories as to the origin of Ecotourism, pointing to different countries and times, and an even greater array of differing definitions.

In Costa Rica the term was initiated and has always been closely related to a company specialized in nature oriented tourism, Tikal Tour Operators. According to Bary Roberts, president of Tikal Tour Operators, which was founded in 1967, he had the priviledge of meeting Dr. Maurice Strong, Undersecretary of the United Nations for Ecological Affairs, a famous conservationsist and the organizer of the 1992 Earth Summit in Rio de Janeiro, in 1978. Together, they discussed the need to transform the traditional form of natural history tourism into an effective educational instrument that would make a significant contribution towards changing the ecological consciousness of the world. To help achieve this, Dr. Strong made a symbolic investment in Tikal Tour Company, designating his Costa Rican firm, called Ecodesarollos S. A., to be his share holder. Once the objectives of their particular tourist program were defined, it was necessary to provide it with a name. Using Dr. Strong's company's name, Ecodesarollos, as a model, Mr. Roberts named this new tourist phenomenon Ecotourism.

As Mr. Roberts explained, at first most people in the industry mocked him and his products' names. However, little by little, they started catching on, to the extent that in 1983

Tikal legally requested its registration as a trademark by the Costa Rican government, trying to prevent others from using the name for different purposes which might discredit the basic objective it was created for. Finally, in 1985, Tikal Tour Operators was able to have Ecotourism inscribed as its registered trademark. It was at about this same time that Mr. Roberts invented the word Ecoadventures, in order to identify the »soft adventure« product line Tikal was offering, with an emphasis in Ecotourism. Other similar names have followed, such as Ecosafari, Ecolodge, etc.

Tikal's definition of ECOTOURISM, in simple terms, is: »a recreational and educational activity that is carried out in full contact with nature, providing people with all the commodities and levels of service that they expect for their hard earned vacations, while making them aware of the fact that they not only enjoyed their stay, but that they actually invested their time wisely. Ecotourism's main objective is to interpret the structures and operating formats of the tropical ecosystems, within the multiple expressions of the natural phenomena. However, Ecotourism is also an integral philosophy that seeks to bring together our natural resources and man's interaction with them, into a responsible and sustainable tourist product.«

Tikal's definition of ECOADVENTURES, also simply put, is: »a variety of sports, and other physical activities, that are carried out in full and direct contact with nature, guided by specialist nature guides that make the natural environment come alive with beauty and meaning. Included in

these activities we find mountain biking, horse back riding, hiking through jungles, windsurfing, snorkeling, cave exploring, scuba diving, etc.«

»A lot of emphasis is placed on the interpretation of the relationship between man and nature, both the negative impact (contamination, deforestation, etc.) and the positive impact (adequate management of our natural resources). We are very proud to state that we have working with us the best team of guides in the country, among them expert biologists, forest engineers, zoologists, etc.«

Costa Rica has become a leading destination worldwide in the Ecotourist and Ecoadventure sectors of the tourist industry, some of the reasons why, as well as some of their basic parameters, being the following:

1) Despite its small geographical extension, the country offers an amazing biological diversity, all distributed in 12 different life zones with inumerable ecosystems.

2) In 1972 Costa Rica founded an excellent National Park System which, coupled with a great number of private and public biological reserves, makes up a paradise for nature lovers and covers more than 32% of the total national territory in a protected area of some sort.

3) The sociological and cultural impact of this kind of specialized tourism is much less severe than that of conventional tourism, due to a strong desire of the client to see and learn more from the host country rather than to impose his own cultural habits. Also, contracting the labor force of each property from the local area avoids and counteracts normal

migration problems and raises the levels of culture and income of the community.

4) The ecological impact of this type of tourism, if responsibly and conscientiously handled, is not only minimal, it should include reforestation and other types of programs that protect and regenerate nature.

5) The financial contribution to the country, as well as the horizontal distribution of this income, is a lot greater with this line of tourism than with conventional tourism, because clients are generally from higher social classes, as well as the fact that they visit more rural areas.

6) Due to the nature of the services of this type of tourism, the investment in infrastructure is much more modest. The essence of naturalist tourism does not require large hotels with lots of facilities, a type of development which negatively affects the natural ambience and the surrounding ecosystems.

Certain operational ethics of Ecotourism are implemented by Tikal Tour Operators, including the following:

– Groups are no larger than 18 people or else get split up.

– Parks and reserves are visited in a cyclical fashion, thus avoiding too much impact on one area. If necessary, when a park or reserve has too large a demand from other sources, overnight stays get limited to day trips at most.

– All services and activities are always conducted and supervised by specialist nature guides, with first – class equipment and all the necessary safety precautions.

– An introductory talk about the natural history of the area and on various aspects related to conservation is part of every tour and helps raise the consciousness of the client.

– The company tries to make all its food suppliers utilize natural foods whenever possible and to always utilize biodegradable, or reusable, packaging for box lunches.

– The accommodation for passengers is most often provided in lodges that are found in areas near the national parks or reserves, but never within them.

– Special attention is paid to the utilization of private biological reserves, whenever possible, in order to increase the offer of destinations available to the natural history tourists, and because their proper use can be regulated much more effectively, the pressure on national parks and reserves can be reduced as well.

– No smoking within the national parks and reserves is allowed for staff and clients. As well, noise is kept down to a minimum level.

– All passengers on the tours are given paper garbage bags for their trash and are requested to help pick up any trash as he or she goes along the trails.

– All passengers are given the opportunity of planting a tree, and are provided with information on ways they can help.

– Particular projects are selected that are oriented towards the protection or regeneration of nature in the areas visited. The company tries to involve each one of its major wholesalers and clients, to make contributions and promote their implementation by getting them to donate some of their profits to these projects as well.

– All the staff is trained, as well as those of the partners in service, to provide an educational background for all the products. Tikal is convinced that the educational emphasis is one of the greatest assets of their products, which gives clients the highest level of satisfaction.

– All the promotional and office materials are gradually being changed over to recycled paper. Partners are being encouraged to do likewise as well.

One of the main objectives of Tikal Tour Operators is to become the leading company in Costa Rica in the management of natural history tourism, and to see that the essentials of our Ecotourist and Ecoadventure products are widely implemented around the country. This will not only benefit us, but also the country as a whole, as it will ensure a national, sustainable tourist product, as well as force a differentiation of our products from those that are simply trying to ride the ecological tourist wave and are not willing to pay the price.

As part of this, we have established the goal of having the great majority of our tours based on private property by the end of 1995, in order to more effectively control the proper use and management of the natural areas. To achieve this, we have been consistently offering incentives to the private sector for developing private biological reserves with lodge-type accommodation, and have started out by doing so ourselves, at our ECOADVENTURE LODGE, which is a most successful and ecologically sound project that we hope will be imitated by others.

ECOTOURISM & ECOADVENTURES are registered trademarks of Agencia de Viajes Tikal S. A.

Practical tips

Money – Costa Rica's currency is the Colón (named after Columbus). US Dollars (Cash or Travelers' Checks) can be changed in banks or hotels. Major credit cards are accepted.

Immigration – United States and Canadian citizens are only required proof of citizenship, although a valid passport is prefered. Most other nationalities are required to have only a valid passport and a tourist permit or visa. Costa Rican consulates should be consulted for the latest immigration regulations.

Vaccinations – Costa Rica does not require any vaccination documents upon entering the country. Malaria occurs only rarely in the Caribbean coastal lowlands; therefore, the advantages and disadvantages of malaria precautions should be discussed with a doctor before any such measures are undertaken. The right clothing and, not to be forgotten, an insect repellent provide additional protection. Hepatitis-A precaution and a tetanus booster vaccination, if necessary, are advisable.

Language – Costa Ricans speak Spanish, however non Spanish-speaking tourists always manage to communicate with the friendly Ticos, who are more than willing to practice their limited English. You can usually find people who speak English in hotels, restaurants and major tourist areas.

Time – Costa Rica is located in the Central Mountain Time zone, except for when daylight saving is implemented.

The Authors

Gerhard Eisenschink, born in 1954 in Regensburg, studied English and Geography. At the same time he maintained a strong interest in photography and photojournalism and also worked as a press photographer. Having spent a long period of study in the United States in 1978, his main interest is now landscape photography. The fotos from his extensive trips have appeared in illustrated books, travel reports and calendars by various publishers in Germany and overseas. His Globetrotter volume »Land der Canyons – Abenteuer-Touren durch den Südwesten der USA« was published by Artcolor. He has been a regular visitor to Costa Rica since 1988.

Peter Thomas, born in 1959, studied Geography, Agricultural Technology, Spanish and Art History in Augsburg. Since 1989 he has been lecturer in Physical Geography at the University of Augsburg. His dissertation and doctoral thesis dealt with the subject of ecological and agricultural questions arising in Costa Rica. The author spent a total of three years in Costa Rica and worked as area advisor for industry and agriculture during his studies. He published a travel guide on Costa Rica, which has become generally recognised as a standard.